THE MOBIUS GUIDES
graphology

THE MOBIUS GUIDES

graphology

RICHARD CRAZE

Copyright © 1994, 2003 by Richard Craze

First published in Great Britain in 2003 by Hodder and Stoughton
A division of Hodder Headline

The right of Richard Craze to be identified as the Author
of the Work has been asserted by him in accordance with the
Copyright, Designs and Patents Act 1988.

A Mobius paperback

10 9 8 7 6 5 4 3 2 1

All rights reserved. No part of this publication may be reproduced, stored in
a retrieval system, or transmitted, in any form or by any means without the
prior written permission of the publisher, nor be otherwise circulated in any
form of binding or cover other than that in which it is published and without
a similar condition being imposed on the subsequent purchaser.

A CIP catalogue record for this title is available from the British Library

ISBN 0 34073475 2

Typeset in Fairfield Light by
Palimpsest Book Production Limited, Polmont, Stirlingshire
Printed and bound in Great Britain by
Mackays of Chatham plc, Chatham, Kent

Hodder and Stoughton
A division of Hodder Headline
338 Euston Road
London NW1 3BH

The author would like to thank all the people who have so kindly donated samples of their handwriting.

contents

introduction x

what is graphology? x

the history of graphology x

how graphology works xi

who uses graphology and why xii

1 how we begin 1
   Obtaining a sample 1
   What you will need 3
   Questions to ask first 3

2 first impressions 6
   Paper 6
   Ink 7
   Pens 9
   Pressure 10
   Margins 11
   Style 14
   Content 14
   Summary 15

3 is size important? — 16

Letter size — 16
Width of words — 18
Space between words — 19
Space between lines — 20
Capital and lower case letters — 20
Starting and finishing strokes — 21
Summary — 23

4 zones — 25

The three zones — 25
Zone traits — 27
How we measure zones — 29
Summary — 30

5 dominant traits — 31

Why are the 'w' and 'd' so important? — 32
Loops — 34
Middle zone letters — 35
Stems — 36
Summary — 37

6 leanings — 38

Slants — 38
Slopes — 41
Does your handwriting change? — 43

7 connections — 47

The garland — 47
The arcade — 48
The angle — 49
The thread — 49
Uncial and cursive handwriting — 50
Legibility — 52

8 letters and numbers — 55

Letters — 55
Major traits of letter groups — 57
Numbers — 62

9 dotting and crossing — 64

Positioning of the 'i' dot — 64
Time for 't's — 68

10 signing off — 72

What does your signature reveal? — 73
Signature same as handwriting — 74
Signature different from handwriting — 75
Placements — 81
Forenames and surnames — 83

11 odds and ends — 86

The capital 'I' — 86
Envelopes — 89
Address placement — 91

12 making an analysis — 93

Suggested procedures — 93
Looking for graphological traits — 94
Looking for character traits — 95

13 samples for practice — 98

The samples — 98
The interpretations — 100

further reading — 109

useful addresses — 110

introduction

What is graphology?

Graphology is the analysis of a person's character from their handwriting. It often reveals a lot that might normally be hidden. At school, we are all taught to write in a similar style, but once we have left we put our own stamp of originality on our writing. The way we shape the individual letters, the way we join them together and the way we create space around our writing are all an unconscious choice that reflects how we feel about ourselves, the environment around us and our relationships with other people. The graphologist is someone trained to know what all these unconscious choices mean in relation to our personality.

The history of graphology

Graphology is not a new science. As early as the seventeenth century, it was studied and written about. The first major work was that of Camillo Baldi, a university professor in Bologna. In 1622, he wrote a book, *The Means of Knowing the Habits and Qualities of a Writer from his Letters*, and his work was expanded over many years.

In Paris in 1872, the Abbé Jean Michon published his books, *The Mysteries of Handwriting*, and *A System of Graphology*. He made up the word *graphology* from the Greek, *grapho*, which means 'I write' and *logos* 'study'. His books generated considerable interest in Europe where the subject was considered worthy enough to warrant further investigation.

The first detailed classification of handwriting was carried out by another Frenchman, Jean Crepieux-Jamin, who established the basic principles of graphology that are still in use today.

In 1925 the Czechoslovakian graphologist, Robert Saudek, came to England and founded the first British journal of graphology, *Character and Personality*. Despite this, we lagged behind somewhat until the middle of this century when academics, escaping from the Nazis, brought their knowledge and skills with them to this country. They included H. J. Jacoby who published his *Analysis of Handwriting: An Introduction into Scientific Graphology* in 1939.

Even today, there is a certain reservation shown towards graphology, either through ignorance or because it has sometimes been used for fortune-telling in fairgrounds.

There is quite an interesting exercise you can do to see what I mean. Look in your *Yellow Pages* under *Graphologists*. You may find one or two names there. But what is more likely is that it will tell you to look under *Hand-Writing Analysts* or, incredibly, to look under *Clairvoyants and Palmists*.

Yet today there are European universities offering graphology degrees, a considerable number of graphology societies, and the USA, always cautious in its assessments, has officially declared it a science.

How graphology works

Graphology has been studied for centuries, and so there is a considerable well-tested body of opinion that forms the basis of modern graphology. The way we form our letters falls into distinct categories that have been shown to indicate various traits in our character. We have to learn these classifications – zones, slants, loops, stems, etc. – and also be able to recognize features in the handwriting that relate to various personality types. Everybody has a personal and identifiable handwriting that is as unique as their fingerprints, and within that handwriting are the clues to their inner self. What we have to do is learn the categories and marry them up with the character traits.

Who uses graphology and why?

Obviously the trained graphologist uses it, but what for? It is being used increasingly in personnel selection, vocational guidance, personality assessment, relationship compatibility, police and forensic work, psychological appraisals, establishing forgeries, identifying anonymous letter writers, verifying authenticity of historical documents and as an interesting and rewarding pastime.

This book aims to teach you the basics of graphology as you follow it step by step. At the end of it you should, exercising the responsibility suited to such a task, be able to assess the basic traits of someone's character. It is not written for someone seeking to study graphology in great depth with the intention of taking it up as a career.

If, after reading this book, you wish to explore graphology further, I recommend you approach the British Institute of Graphology, the International Graphology Analysis Society or the Graphology Society for details of courses leading to a professional qualification (addresses are listed at the back of the book under *Further information*).

In addition, this book should also encourage you to develop your powers of observation. To enter the field of character analysis presupposes an interest in people. I trust that this book will help further that interest and provide you with a considerable amount of fun along the way.

All the samples of handwriting used have been reduced to approximately three quarters of their actual size, so please bear this in mind in the sections where size is a factor in your interpretation and you are trying to assess what 'normal' size is.

1

how we begin

So, now we are ready to begin. We are about to learn how to analyse someone's character from their handwriting. What is the first thing we will need? That is right – some handwriting. But what sort? Well, you already have friends and relatives, so now is the time to start making use of them.

You already know their personalities quite well, and they are all quite nice, generous and kind people otherwise you would not be friends with them, right? So ask them for a sample of their writing.

Obtaining a sample

An A4 size page is best. Get them to write you a letter, that way you will be able to see how they use space, where they put the address and so on. Also you will get a large sample and, probably

Graphology

most importantly, get to see their signature.

You should stress that fact that their writing should be as natural as possible.

And you should endeavour to have them use the pen/ink that they would normally write with. It is handy when you are starting out to have several samples in front of you all on an A4 sheet, as you can then compare widths and heights, etc.

Although an A4 sheet would be best for your needs, you must not impose on their need to express their inner self, after all that is what graphology is all about. If they usually write on blue-lined notepaper or use the backs of old envelopes, then be more than happy to have those as samples. They will tell you more than you might have otherwise learnt if you had insisted on conformity.

Such a sample may look like this:

> 32, Hanover Street
> Fishmouth
> Rutland
> RB27 8LT
>
> Dear Susannah
>   I'm so glad you've decided to take up graphology, and here's a sample of my handwriting — I've kept it as natural as I can.
>   I hope it all goes well for you — knife-throwing was never really you. Not with your eyesight, anyway.
>   Regards,
>   Nathaniel.

Handwriting sample.

Perhaps you already have such samples. Do you keep correspondence? If not, now is the time to start.

You need a certain amount of respect for the writer. Make sure you have their permission before you start analysing the writing.

What you will need

- A good quality magnifying glass is an absolute necessity.
- A transparent ruler clearly marked in inches and centimetres. This is for measuring line spacing, gaps between words, etc.
- A protractor for measuring the angles of loops and stems.
- A set of files to keep the samples in.

Questions to ask first

Graphology is not a method of psychic investigation or guesswork or fortune-telling. It is an exact and respectable science. If you went to a doctor, you would be expected to tell them where you had the pain, what your symptoms were, how long you had had them for, and any previous similar ailments. It would be necessary for them to have this information in order to be able to make a diagnosis.

Similarly, as a graphologist, you will need to have certain information to be able to proceed to a correct interpretation. Do not be tempted by people who try to lure you into demonstrating your skill as a sort of party trick. I am sure you know what I mean. Someone will hand you a piece of paper with a few words scrawled on it and then expect you to be able to tell them everything about the person who wrote it. Do not be tempted.

Before you can begin an analysis you will need to know if the sample comes from a man or a woman, adult or child. This is important information because people's writing sometimes does not reflect their sex or age, and you will need to know these in advance to stop you making assumptions. Some men's writing can appear very feminine and some women's can come across as extremely masculine. In addition, older people's writing often takes on a childlike quality. If you attempt to analyse a child's writing, you will need several samples taken over a period of time as their writing tends to change quite frequently and dramatically.

For all samples you need to know the following: the age, sex, nationality, and the 'handedness' of the writer. The last piece of information is important as letter formations will be different for left-and right-handed people and you could make an incorrect assumption if you did not know with which hand they wrote.

You will probably need some system of record keeping if you are to carry this through successfully. A simple sheet that lists all the relevant information could be as follows:

NAME	AGE
SEX	LEFT/RIGHT
NATIONALITY	STATUS
DATES OF SAMPLES	COMMENTS
ANALYSIS	
VERIFICATION	

Record sheet.

The verification part is important as you will need to know if your interpretations are along the right lines to begin with. That is why it is best to use friends at first, as you already have something to go by.

Later you can get different friends to submit samples without you knowing who they are from. That way you will be able to put your abilities to the test.

You will also need some practice in writing character assessments. They should be concise and clear such as:

The writer shows a good strong character with some signs of tiredness. There is optimism and energy, but also a tendency towards being stubborn and headstrong. The lower margins indicate a submerged emotional distance that is also reflected elsewhere. Although the writer seems to be energetic and open, there are clues that something is amiss, perhaps too great a need for praise and encouragement. Mature and good at making decisions but there are signs of depression with a tendency to lose heart at minor obstacles.

Writing reports takes time to master, so practise. You need to look for signs of being: optimistic/pessimistic, depressive/manic, headstrong/weak-willed, mature/immature, decisive/indecisive, introvert/extrovert, etc. Later chapters will explore these signs in more detail.

So, now you have your samples and tools, you are ready to begin. But first, here are a few questions to see how much you remember from what you have read in this first chapter.

Practice

- What is graphology?
- What sort of sample should you ask for?
- What tools will you need?
- What questions should you ask first?
- What records should you keep?
- Why is verification important?

2
first impressions

Having obtained a suitable sample of handwriting, you are now ready to begin your analysis.

Paper

If your sample is not on A4 paper, spend some time feeling the paper; your subject chose it and it tells you something already. Is it fine-quality writing paper? Tatty note paper? White A4 typewriter paper? We can gain an impression from these examples alone. The first type of paper means they care about impressions, the second means they do not, while the third means they have artistic or creative leanings (or are obedient).

By using your own powers of observation, you can begin to feel a lot about your subject from the paper.

When he was younger, my brother always wrote on brown paper – yes, correspondence as well! What does that tell you about him? A need to be very different? To stand out? Artistic? Imaginative? Well, he is now stage director for a theatre in London that specializes in experimental work.

If questioned, subjects will always come up with various reasons why they use particular paper or pens, but usually these are excuses. The fact is, they chose them – it is as simple as that. Our unconscious has an unnerving habit of surfacing when we least expect it. Graphology is about taking those clues and making an interpretation from them. Ignore the excuses, use your powers of observation and remember that graphology is not a fairground trick.

If it were, then some nine universities in Germany would not be offering degree courses in it, would they?

Look at the overall impression the page gives you. Is the writing neat or scrawled, childlike or well formed? Compare it with the person who wrote it. Are they the same or does their writing reveal a hidden side of them? You may often find it does.

Ink

Now turn your attention to the colour of the ink. The general range includes black, blue, grey, green, red, and purple. Your subject chose that colour . . . now let us find out why: what they are trying to tell *us* from that choice? Read the first two examples and then, when you read the rest, try to decide what the colours might mean before you read the interpretation. Graphology is as much about developing your powers of observation as it is about learning whole lists of meanings parrot fashion. You have to do some of the work as well!

Black
Depends on the intensity, but this is usually used by the more

serious types of subjects; the darker the shade the more seriously they take themselves.

Turquoise
The lighter the shade, the more the subject leans towards a spiritual approach to life. Turquoise is a harmonious colour.

Black-blue
This is used by business people who are fairly conventional and serious. They like to blend in and not stand out; they are masculine and conventional.

Mid-blue
This implies a desire to impress. Often this colour is used by men to express their feminine side and by women to express their male side. They have artistic leanings, but they may be tempered by conformity.

Royal-blue
A strong colour chosen by subjects who are sure of themselves, know their direction and are usually quite happy with their position in life. The same comments apply as with the mid-blue concerning the expression of masculinity and femininity.

Grey
Used by musicians and writers, or subjects who have those aspirations. They can show a tendency towards depression and/or seriousness.

Brown
Artists, writers and graphic designers go for brown when they have achieved a measure of success in their lives. Younger, less-successful subjects using this colour may have an over-inflated opinion of themselves.

Green
Could be considered artistic – a desire to be seen as different – but it often covers a strong inferiority complex or lack of emotional stability.

Red
A colour chosen by professional types: bankers, lawyers, accountants, headmasters, etc. It implies a degree of pomposity. Non-professional people using this colour are expressing a warmth and vitality and a need to express the more physical side of their nature. (And how do we tell if they are non-professional people? That comes from content, style and further examination.)

Purple
Quite the opposite of the green-ink users. Green and purple are almost opposite colours and the types of subjects that choose them will be almost opposite as well. This colour indicates an over-developed sense of the subject's own importance and superiority – they need to be seen as above or better than others.

Remember not to jump to too many conclusions yet. We are looking for clues at this stage. The clues may be misleading and we need to check many things before making an interpretation.

Pens

It does not take much practice to begin to tell the types of pens used: italic, biro, fountain pen, etc. Some people even use pencils (they are the true eccentrics). Look at the way the letters are formed and you will see the type of pen that formed them. What does each type of pen tell us? Artistic subjects choose artistic pens – the italic pen, the drawing pen, in other words, the unusual. Practical types choose sensible fountain pens. Those with a need to impress choose the more expensive fountain pens. With a very little practice you will be able to tell when an expensive pen has been used. There is something about the way the ink flows, it has a sort of natural quality to it that fairly jumps off the page at you. Rushed, hurried types pick up whatever is to hand, and that means it is usually a biro – sticky, cheap and a tendency to smudge. Are they like that too?

Look at the overall shape of the letters. The nib made them. Are they wide or narrow? Is the ink smooth and warm, or harsh and even, like a biro. You can tell what pen and nib were used just by looking.

Pressure

Begin by turning the page over. What shows through? Anything? Nothing? Most subjects will fall somewhere in between – just the right sort of pressure. But there are many who will use excessive or too little pressure, irrespective of the surface they are writing on.

Excessive pressure
Aggressive, irritable, impulsive, obstinate, stubborn, thoughtless.

Heavy pressure
Energetic, decisive, tenacious, powerful, vital, determined, controlled, masculine.

Light pressure
Tolerant, sensitive, caring, nurturing, receptive, modest, aware, feminine, adaptable.

Too Light pressure
Timid, weak, depressed, passive, lacking in energy.

No surprises there. But remember these are clues only. No snap assessments. Make your notes and the clues may begin to point you in the right direction. You can start to put together various factors now. For example, if your subject is using green ink and light pressure, you may be right in thinking you have a fairly sensitive, artistic writer, but you need some more detail before making an analysis.

Margins

The margins reflect the space we like to leave around ourselves. We are the writing in the middle telling the world to stay back or that it is all right to come a little closer. Look at your sample page. Does the writing sit comfortably in the middle? Does it feel balanced?

Left margin

We start writing at the left-hand margin, choosing the point at which to begin communicating with the outside world. At this moment, our unconscious is making a statement about how we feel about the world around us. Do we hug the top, left-hand corner because we feel insecure, or do we leave a reasonable space both above and to the left because we feel well adjusted and confident in ourselves? Or do we leave too wide a space indicating pride and reserve?

If the margin starts out well but widens towards the bottom of the page, it can indicate a form of inner tiredness – we have not the will to keep the effort going. If it narrows, we are prudent and can pace our energy well, maybe too well – we could do with a little more spontaneity.

The left margin is the control. We chose where it starts and how it flows. It expresses how we feel we relate to the world. There is no standard width that is right or wrong. *You* must feel if it is comfortable depending on the size of page and size of writing. We are looking for harmony and balance. The clues are there when the harmony and balance are missing.

Right margin

The right margin forms itself. It has less control and can reflect our approach to life. A lack of right margin indicates vitality and rushing forward without looking.

A wide right margin shows timidity – we are not anxious to face change and the future. The right margin should be a little narrower than the left. If the left and right margins are balanced, and the upper and lower margins are balanced too, you have a rare subject indeed – this is often a sign of advanced spiritual thinking, a knowledge of life and death, a deep thinker who is isolated and reserved.

Upper margin

Look at the top right corner. What appears there? The address? Is it printed or written? What does that tell you?

A wide upper margin indicates the conventional, modest and respectful. A narrow upper margin tends to come from selfish or indifferent subjects. They are unable to see the visual impact their communication makes upon the world – or do not care if it offends by its lack of harmony.

Lower margin

Narrow lower margins indicate thoughtful subjects – good communicators who speak their words carefully. They can be a little introspective, and if the margin disappears altogether they can tend towards depression.

Wide lower margins indicate aloof types who like to keep their space intact. You will not get emotionally close to them and the wide lower margin is their 'Keep Out' sign.

No margins

If you remember to see the page as the world and the writing as the person, then subjects leaving no margins are filling the entire universe with themselves. Luckily, these types are rare. They are usually lovable, but may not be that popular as they tend to bounce in upon you with little thought for your need for privacy or respect for other's space.

> 4-7, King Street
> Emsbury
> Northants.
> N912 8SF.
>
> Dear Robin
> Many thanks for your letter — it was lovely to hear from you.
> I've been quite busy since I last wrote, decorating the house. Unfortunately the ceiling in the hall fell down last October, and part of it landed on my head. I spent a night in hospital with concussion, worrying about having to clear up

Well-proportioned margins.

> = everyone shopping in street
> entire Britain population & trade.
> entire population of britain
>
> a fraction of the population that you survey must have a large enough sample to obtain an accurate result.
> larger the sample, more accurate result.
> - but too large a sample makes processing difficult.

No margins.

Style

By now you will have gained a lot from just holding the page, examining the paper and the ink and looking at the margins. You will have had a chance to get to know the page quite well.

What impression of your subject have you formed? Look at the style. Is it well balanced or scruffy? Does it please you or do you feel some strange dislike of it? People are very similar to their writing. Those that are well adjusted, happy people have well-adjusted, happy writing. Those who are unpleasant, corrupt, aggressive or emotionally flawed, will probably have writing that reflects their inner turmoil.

You are obviously a sensitive soul yourself with a need to understand and help people or you would not be reading and learning from this book. As a sensitive soul, you will have a natural affinity with people and your powers of observation will be strong. Look at the page. What do you get from it? Does it seem wholesome or is there some oddness about it that somehow does not feel quite right.

Style gives us an overall impression and we can learn much about our subject from it.

Content

Most conventional graphologists will tell you content is not relevant. I could not disagree more. Take time now to actually read what you have in front of you. Read it and it will tell you much about your subject. Their education, their social background, their communication abilities, their zest for life. It is all there in the content.

Is it legible? Do they want you to read what they have written and, if not, why not? We write for others to read unless we are scribbling notes to ourselves. Illegible writing could be the result of any one of a number of things: lack of consideration;

extreme intelligence; or severe emotional problems. Again you will have to look for clues elsewhere to verify which of these it is; it may be that the writer is writing faster than normal. What does that tell you?

Summary

I will leave you to use your skills to draw what conclusions you can from the content and then add them to the clues already drawn from the paper, ink, margins and style. By now you may know your subject quite well and we have not even looked at a single letter yet! That is next, but ask yourself these few practice questions before you go on.

Practice

- What would it tell you if someone usually wrote on blue lined paper?
- What does it tell us about a person if they use turquoise ink?
- Who would use excessive pressure?
- What sort of margins would Tigger leave?
- What clues would wide upper margins give you?
- What does style tell you?

3

is size important?

Size is probably the first thing we notice about a person's writing. It is the most visual sign of how the writer feels about themselves and, as such, must figure quite highly in our appraisals.

Letter size

How do we assess size? There is obviously no standard, but it has been found that writing around 9 mm overall from top to bottom is a useful gauge of *medium*. This allows 3 mm each for loops, middle letters and stems.

Medium writing
People whose writing falls into the medium category (and having normally well-balanced writing) like to conform. They tend to be conservative in their outlook.

> A good year for
> she has shown that she has
> the ability and determination
> to do well in this subject.

Medium-size writing.

Large writing

Large writing is any that extends beyond the 9 mm range.

> all the treeble!
> been caused JJ

Large writing.

The large writers are bold and expressive. They like to make an impression in the world and be clearly seen. It is the mark of the egotist and show-off. They may be showing signs of conceit and arrogance. They may, however, be genuinely 'bigger' people than most, the Gengis Khans of the world, people who make an impact.

Graphology

Small writing

Small is defined as any writing that falls significantly below the 9 mm range.

> One of the reasons I'm writing this is because I feel, did me a real service when I was going through way. You gave me your love, your interest, your

Small writing.

Small writing is a reflection of how the person sees themselves. Perhaps introvert and inward turning. It can, however, indicate someone who thinks a lot. They are able to concentrate their ideas and efforts into a small space and have the ability to see an entire problem in one go, unlike the large writer who often overlooks details.

Width of words

This is not to be confused with the space between words. It is the breadth of each word. A standard is found for each sample by taking the letter 'n'. The distance between the two downstrokes should be roughly the height of one of them. This gives you a standard to work with.

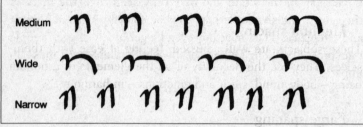

How to measure width.

Medium width
Moderate people use a medium width. They tend to be the same subjects as the ones who use the medium-size letters. If there is a marked difference you need to probe further.

Wide width
Happy-go-lucky people tend to enlarge their words. They are spontaneous, cheerful and relaxed, anxious to get on with it and be on to the next idea.

Narrow width
Here we find someone holding themselves in, reserved and controlled. Perhaps a little emotionally uptight and unable to relax. They can be self-conscious, even withdrawn.

Space between words

Remember the example given earlier of the writing being the person? Well, the individual words themselves represent the component parts of the human being. The space between them is how they feel about their completeness. We measure the space between words by taking an average from the sample in front of us. Could you insert the word *an* in between each word using the sample's letter size? That is a rough guide. You may be able to quickly spot large and narrow spacing at a glance.

Medium spacing
These subjects are well adjusted, feeling at ease with themselves. They see the necessity of all the elements of a human being – body, mind, spirit and emotions – in harmony.

Large spacing
These subjects have a looser connection with themselves,

perhaps overlooking some vital part. You can usually find out which part from other clues in their writing.

Narrow spacing
This can be an indication of the subject being too concerned with themselves, worrying over every detail.

Space between Lines

The space between lines represents our approach to other people. Too wide and we tend to be reserved and distant. Too narrow and we tend to be clingy – needing people around us all the time. As a rough guide, you should be able to insert another line of writing in the space.

If the writing is large, with loops and stems overlapping the line above or below, the subject acts very much on their feelings, makes snap decisions and can be impulsive.

Similarly, when the writing is small and the lines between also small, there may be emotional confusion, the subject being unable to separate their feelings from the reality of a situation.

Capital and lower case letters

The relationship between capitals and lower case letters is another important area to look at.

Large capitals
Where the capital letter is larger than the writing and extends well into the upper zone and is also out of proportion to the other letters, it can indicate a feeling of superiority. They may well have an overrated opinion of themselves. Forceful, proud and arrogant are all words that could be applied.

> *Happy Birthday darling.*
> *Easter. All my love*

Large capitals.

Small capitals

If the capitals are noticeably too small compared to the lower case letters, it can indicate submissiveness and a general lack of confidence, but it may also be an indication of modesty or an ability to concentrate. As in all areas, you will need to look elsewhere for verification of any assessments you are making.

> *So money is OK. We students*
> *get money and discounts from*
> *(Nat west - £400 interest free loan*

Small capitals.

Starting and finishing strokes

The first mark we make upon a blank page may be the most significant. We choose (usually without it being a conscious decision) where and how we make that mark. It is the beginning of our attempt to communicate with the outside world and represents our ideas and ambitions. It is known as the

Graphology

initial stroke and should be looked for at the beginning of each sentence, paragraph and page.

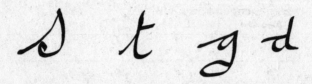

Initial strokes.

Initial strokes

If you look at the initial stroke, it will usually form the start of a capital letter. If it starts below the rest of the letter or writing, the subject may well be self-opinionated, even moody and bad tempered; a barely formed initial stroke usually indicates intelligence and quick thinking – they already want to get on with the rest of the word.

Unlike many adults, children invariably make clearly defined initial strokes. I am sure you can work out how you can use that information if you have an adult who uses clearly defined initial strokes a lot.

Watch out for excessively long initial strokes as they are a good indicator of someone who is not as self-assured as they would have you believe. It may be a sign of pride though, so look for confirmation elsewhere.

Terminal strokes

How we finish our words is very revealing because we cannot choose the final letter of any word, so we have to form the terminal unconsciously. It is the best indicator of our humane side: do we give or are we selfish, generous or mean? Look for the terminal stroke on the 'e'. If it is cut off short, we do not like

Is Size Important?

to give too much. A long terminal indicates a generous nature, but if it curls upwards the subject is likely to be taken advantage of.

Terminals that end in a thickening or very blunt way show signs of resentment and even hostility.

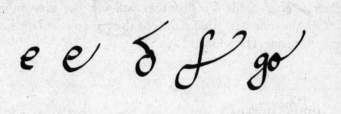

Terminal strokes.

If you want to know what someone's manners are like, look at the end of their 'y's. Abrupt endings indicate abrupt, even rude, people. If you find you have a 'y' with a long and elegant sweep, then you are dealing with one of life's natural charmers.

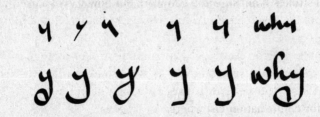

Rude 'y's and polite 'y's.

Summary

I have covered a lot of ground in this chapter. Next we move on to the dominant traits, but make sure you have taken in everything in this chapter first. Remember to gauge the overall impression of size first before you move on to the detailed areas. It will be obvious when something looks out of place or wrong. 'Nicely-formed' people have nicely formed writing. Look for discrepancies. Look for oddities and then delve further. And if you want some more training, get your friends to try and disguise their writing. Odds are that they will disguise everything – except the terminals. That is the one thing people find the hardest to change. Have fun!

Practice

- How do we measure size?
- What is defined as large writing?
- How do we measure width?
- What does narrow spacing between words tell us?
- Why should we look out for excessively long initial strokes?
- What would we look at to determine manners?
- What do we find the hardest to disguise in our writing?

4

zones

In Chapter 3 we dealt with size, and it was suggested that 9 mm was an average measurement to work with. The 9 mm can be further broken down into three segments of 3 mm each. These are known as the three zones.

The Three Zones

Upper zone

This is the top segment of the three. This is where we look when we want to find out about the subject's intellectual, spiritual and imaginative powers. This is where they keep their aspirations and dreams.

We cannot just look at the letter formations in the upper zone in isolation. It is always a question of balance: of looking for the odd or out of place. Anything large or strangely formed should stand out at once. We should also compare anything in the upper zone with the other two zones to see if there is an imbalance. Also check capital letters to see how far they enter the upper zone, their size in relationship to the lower case letters, their style, etc.

Letters in the upper zone.

The upper zone can be seen as the higher self, the noble side of our nature.

Middle zone

This zone reflects our everyday life. This is the place to look to see how subjects cope with reality: how they socialize and relate to others. Again look for the oddities. Extreme size or pressure can indicate a need to dominate; while letters that are smaller than those in the other zones can indicate someone who feels suppressed.

Middle-zone letters.

Lower zone

This is the place to see how the subject relates to sex, instinct, the subconscious, their inner desires, the hidden side of their nature.

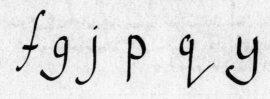

Lower-zone letters.

Zone traits

By looking at which zone is dominant, we can gather clues as to their character traits. This can determine the basic type of person we are working with. Traits can have a negative or positive quality, so we will need to look elsewhere in the writing for confirmation, but if the writing is odd or looks wrong in a particular zone, then it may well be the negative quality that is being revealed. Conversely, if the writing is pleasing to the eye, well rounded and in proportion, then it is probably the positive side that is being emphasized. Obviously, these classifications are very subjective and, as you gain experience, you will draw up your own list.

Upper-zone traits

Positive: Perfectionism, free thinking, independence, ambitious, intellectual, spiritually in tune, shows a wide range of interests, high ideals, logical thinking, at ease with themselves.

Negative: Remote, cut off from reality, undisciplined, erratic, forgetful, attracted to the weird and wonderful, unable to see ideas through.

Predominantly upper zone.

Middle-zone traits

Positive: Firm, determined, practical, well adjusted, capable, reliable, realistic, truthful, honest.

Negative: Petulant, self-opinionated, dogged, obstinate, stubborn, unable to accept criticism, dominating, materialistic, dishonest, untruthful, calculating.

Predominantly middle zone.

Lower-zone traits

Positive: Stable, sensible, at ease with their own sexuality, well mannered, sensual, wholesome, graceful.

Negative: Sexually bizarre or unduly repressed, does not adapt easily, devious, narcissistic, conceited, ostentatious, vain, cruel.

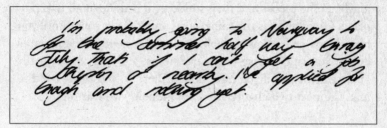

Predominantly lower zone.

As you can see, there is quite a variety. Remember we are in the business of analysing, not judging. Try to keep your assessments as objective as you can; after all, someone writing predominantly in the lower zone, and showing all the negative qualities, could actually be of another type entirely.

How we measure zones

We have our basic standard of 3 mm per zone. This works well for standard-size writing. However, if the writing is very large or very small, we may need to adjust that measurement. You still would need to find a standard that would be divisible by three. It is the relationship of the zones to each other rather than a specific measurement. You have to compare each zone: is one predominantly larger or smaller? It is best to get in the habit of judging these things visually rather than only gauging by measurement.

Remember to visually divide the writing into thirds; if it fits into the 3 mm/9 mm range, it is easier for you. But if it does not, do not worry, just work harder.

Summary

I trust you now have an understanding of the three zones. Graphology is a bit like a child's interlocking puzzle. You have to juggle all the pieces and then suddenly it is done; it all falls into place. Graphology is the same: you cannot cover zones until you have loops and stems to look at, and you need to learn slants before you can analyse loops and stems, and you cannot really analyse slants until you have done zones. So you really need to read the next two chapters in conjunction with this one.

Practice

- What are the three zones?
- How do we measure them?
- What do each of them represent?
- How do we determine which zone a writer uses?
- What are the positive upper zone traits?
- What are the negative middle zone traits?

5

dominant traits

Graphologists will often be asked to assess people's suitability for various forms of employment. They are asked to prepare reports concerning someone's ability to communicate, or how they would fare under pressure, or how honest they are likely to be.

There are important aspects of writing that we should now study to flesh out the interpretation already being established. We have done the ground work. Now we have to start the detail.

We will begin to examine individual letters and have a look at loops and stems.

Why are the 'w' and 'd' so important?

When we want to find out how much of an introvert or extrovert the subject is, then we really need look no further than the 'w'.

Graphology

When you know this basic detail, you can go on to examine other factors to confirm your analysis.

The 'w'

When the end stroke of the 'w' turns inward it is introversion we are seeing, and the reverse is true: a forward end stroke is the sign of the extrovert.

This also gives a good indication to job suitability: you would not recommend an introverted person for the role of sales manager, would you? And the cheerful, outgoing extrovert might not enjoy a job dominated by technology rather than by contact with people.

Introversion and extroversion.

The 'd'

Now you have found out how outgoing your subject is, you will need confirmation. This is where the 'd' comes in: the 'd' should show the same characteristics as the 'w' – inward end stroke indicates introversion; the forward facing end stroke indicates extroversion. But the introverted 'd' will be much more analytical and methodical, careful and patient. The extrovert 'd' will lack organizing skills, could be impulsive, but decisive and sociable.

Dominant Traits

Watch out for 'd's with loops. These can indicate conceit and vanity and someone that needs to be encouraged and praised a lot.

So, you have got a subject who has a forward 'w' and a backward 'd'. You have a thoughtful intelligent subject who will thrive in a creative industry but probably shuns the limelight themselves. This could be (depending on other factors) the handwriting of the film director, the writer, the producer.

Forward 'w', backward 'd'.

Backward 'w' and forward 'd'? This is the person to go to for advice: consultants, advisers, perhaps even priests. These people can cope with the public quite well, but they do need to work closely with a script or some form of ritual.

Backward 'w', forward 'd'.

Graphology

Loops

We can get a good indication of a subject's intelligence by looking at their loops; these are the letters: b, d, h, k, l and t.

Always go for the 'l' first. This letter is the most revealing sign of how the subject's mind works and can indicate levels of emotional stability. The upper zone is also where we would look for spiritual aspirations.

Well-rounded loops

These are made by well-rounded people who are sociable and enthusiastic about life. They are happy to show their feelings and are able to articulate them.

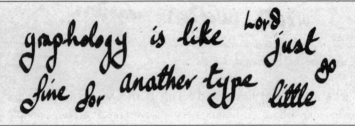

Well-rounded loops.

Well-rounded loops that reach to the top of the upper zone indicate imaginative, thoughtful subjects.

If the loops extend beyond the upper zone, you have an idealist with strong spiritual inclinations. The thinner and taller the loops the higher the aspirations.

Narrow loops

These indicate the logical thinker, the pragmatic realist. Narrow loopers have a black-and-white approach, ideal for forensic scientists and graphologists.

Narrow loops.

No loops

No loops at all denotes someone who does not daydream or fantasize.

No loops.

Middle-zone letters

This is where we look for the subject's approach to day-to-day life. Small letters here can indicate someone who is not really in touch with the practicalities of everyday reality. These subjects can be intense thinkers, dreamers who opt out.

Large, round letters in the middle zone indicate subjects who like to party. They are sociable and popular and their fridges are always full.

Thin, middle-zone letters are used by people well grounded

in the world. They may have a problem with boredom as they are frequently unable to amuse themselves.

Stems

Letters that drop down into the lower zone are called stemmed letters. Imagine them as the root of a plant; the middle zone letters are the body and the upper zone the flower.

Stalks and stems grow up from the ground, the basics. And this is what the stems reveal to us: the instinct. This is where to look if you want to find out about sex.

The letters to look for are: g, j, q, y and z.

Short stems

Blunt types, firm and determined. You will not be able to con them.

Medium stems

Practical and responsible. They know how to make decisions and can be logical and methodical.

Long stems

Strong and idealistic. They know what they want and go for it.

Looped stems

Dreamers and romantics. Usually charming, but you will not be able to pin them down. They like to travel and are always ready to try new experiences. If the looped stem slants backwards, it can indicate emotional disturbances, especially if the loop is much larger than any of the rest of the handwriting.

If the looped stem slopes forward and is very large, it is a sign of a warm and passionate sexual nature. You may have found a Don Juan's handwriting in among your samples.

Dominant Traits

> graphology is an important subject
> graphology is an important subject
> graphology is an important subject
> graphology is an important subject

Short, medium, long and looped stems.

Summary

So, now that we have explored aspects of dominant traits, it is time to go on to slants. Make sure that any interpretations you have made so far are held over until you have more information to go on. Do not rush to conclusions yet: there will be plenty of time for that later.

Practice

- What does the 'w' tell us?
- What does the 'd' tell us?
- Where would we look for signs of intelligence?
- Would you catch Spock using loops?
- And if not, why not?
- Where do we look for sexual expression?

6

leanings

We are taught at school to shape our letters in a fairly upright manner. The instant we are freed from supervision we start to express our individuality. One area that visually communicates our personality well is the way we choose to slant our writing. The slant is the way the individual letters lean, either backwards or forwards (to the left or to the right).

Slants

The measurement for average slants has been established as roughly 45° from the vertical; more than 45° is seen as extreme.

Handwriting is considered to be upright if it is up to 5° either side of vertical.

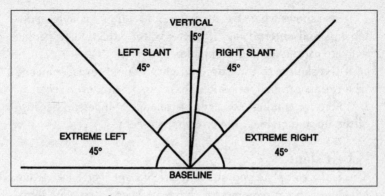

How to gauge slants.

Right slant

If we use the analogy of the writing being ourselves, what does the forward or right slant tell us? That we reach forward? Look forward? Are eager and cheerful? That we reach out to others? That we look to the future with optimism? A right slant can reveal this optimism.

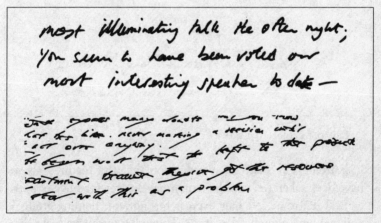

Right and extreme right slants.

Graphology

It also shows where we are active, masculine, sociable, spontaneous and enterprising. It shows warm, affectionate people who are expressive and adaptable.

If the slant is to the extreme right, it could reveal someone who is uncontrolled, impatient, hasty, impulsive, even reckless. It is here we can look for signs of violence in a person because of the unpredictable, excitable temperament.

Left slant

This is the complete opposite of the right slant. The backward or left slant is not as common as the right. These people are introspective and controlled, reserved and cautious. They hold on to the past and are sometimes quite fearful of the future. But it can also be where we express our feminine side, so again look for further clues elsewhere in the writing before reaching conclusions.

Left and extreme left slants.

Extreme left slant is an indication that the features above have been taken too far. The writer may be over-sensitive or even cynical. Extreme left may express resentment, holding grudges and inability to forgive past hurts. The writer may have had a disturbed childhood and have been forced into rigid behaviour patterns. These subjects may be unemotional and cold, or timid and shy. It all points to extreme character behaviour and you need to delve further to pinpoint exactly what it indicates.

Uprights
Completely vertical letters are rare. Allow 5° either side of the vertical line to ascertain uprights. These writers are independent and reliable; they have good self-control and a well-developed sense of direction: they know where they are going and expect to get there.

Slopes

The slope of a subject's writing is defined as the angle at which it lies to the baseline. Does it ascend above a horizontal baseline? Or does it descend below a horizontal baseline? Does it ascend or descend smoothly or in a stepped way? These are all important clues as to our mental and emotional state.

Even if the subject uses lined paper, the trait can still be seen, sometimes the writing overlapping the lines, sometimes rising above them.

Straight
These people are usually stable. It is difficult to unsettle them; they are only thrown off course by real trauma rather than imaginary. They like pleasure and are relaxed and balanced in emotional relationships.

Ascending
These subjects are volatile and excitable, prone to over-indulgence and impulsiveness. They are quick to respond, lively and cheerful. If the writing ascends extremely, they may be prone to rashness, hot tempered and uncontrolled passion.

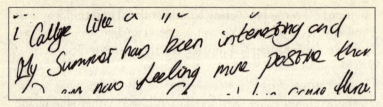

Ascending handwriting.

Stepped ascending
These subjects are showing signs of attempting to curb their over-excitability. They know they can be annoying to others and, as they grow older, are making a genuine effort to be more mature and responsible, and maybe even curbing an over-zealous love life.

Descending
A sign of mental exhaustion or despondency. These subjects are tired, sometimes depressed. They can be moody and secretive. It is often seen in the handwriting of adolescents, especially the ones who are not rebelling openly (it can be an early sign of drug abuse). In adults, descending handwriting is often a very real sign of depression and pessimism.

Descending handwriting.

Stepped descending
This is a good sign that the subject is fighting to overcome natural despondent tendencies. It can often be seen in the

writing of people recovering from disturbed emotional states.

Does your handwriting change?

When we are first taught to write we are influenced by the teacher. As we progress through school, the teachers change and so we get to experience different influences. However, most of those influences will encourage neatness, legibility and formal, stylized presentation. We are writing more for others than for ourselves. When we leave school and begin to express our personalities in a more individual fashion, our handwriting reflects that change.

Our writing develops as we move towards adulthood. It is interesting to compare an adult's handwriting with that of a sample from their earlier years, especially their mid-teens.

Handwriting of a teenager.

Same subject when adult.

In the adolescent writing, we can see the character that is being formed. If the development seems curiously different or stunted,

Graphology

we can expect the subject to have suffered some trauma between the samples. A teenager being suddenly orphaned or their parents divorcing will often arrest the development; the embryonic writing not having been allowed to reach its full maturity.

Even as an adult, your writing will continue to change as you adapt to the changing conditions of your own life.

On a daily basis, it is possible to see changes. Especially in the slope and slant of writing. Tiredness or sudden elation will produce marked changes. However, subjects prone to mood swings will probably have already shown such signs. Maybe their writing is already slightly erratic. Those who are more balanced and less predisposed to mood fluctuations will already reflect that in their handwriting. But we are all at the mercy of outside events. Given any major illness, trauma, stress, bereavement, long-term relationships ending or serious environmental changes, we would expect to see these influences reflected in the writing. That is why it is always helpful to try and get samples from subjects written over a period of time.

Subject suffering severe depression.

Same subject after recovering.

Our writing will probably change depending on whom we are writing for. A note for ourselves will usually be hastily scribbled while a formal job application will be well written, presentable and more effort will have been put into it. The basic characteristics will possibly not change very much, and it would be helpful to have a sample of both sorts of writing.

Our writing also changes on a daily basis if we are writing under the influence of alcohol or drugs, or if we are tired or overworked.

It can be interesting to try practising your own writing and seeing if you can get it to change. When we are younger we all practise our signatures until we develop one that we are happy with, one that seems to serve our purposes: to express our creativity or to impress others with our maturity. Try doing the same with your overall style. After all, if you are reading this book you are showing an interest, are prepared to learn, adaptable and intelligent. Your writing probably already reflects all of these qualities, but it will not hurt to experiment. People who practise are evidently those who wish to improve, and prepared to make an effort and are interested. Those who do not are often uninterested in what people think, either through indifference to other people or because they are prepared to settle for second best. Or maybe it just would not occur to them that *how* they write makes just as much of a statement as *what* they write.

In summary, your writing does change, both in the long term and the short term. If you wish to practise graphology effectively, you must gather as many samples of handwriting as you can. Try to get your subjects to provide you with samples that cover different periods of their lives and written under differing emotional pressures.

Graphology

Practice

- How do we gauge slants?
- What does a right slant reveal?
- What about an extreme right slant?
- If you came across a sample with stepped ascending writing what could you determine about the writer?
- Does your handwriting change, and under what circumstances?

connections

When we first learn to write we form the letters separately. With increasing speed and experience, we begin to join the letters together to form complete words. This joining together is called the connection in graphology.

The connection we choose (consciously or unconsciously) indicates our subconscious thought patterns, our motivations. There are four types of connection and each has a different method of construction that represents our spontaneity and fluency in life.

The garland

The garland connection.

The garland takes two movements of the pen to make. A down and an up stroke. Try it for yourself.

The subjects using this form of connection are practical and natural. There is little guile about them. They are open and honest. The cup-like formation of the garland is full and smooth, well rounded and loving. The subjects are easy going, sincere and sociable, kind and tolerant. They like the pleasures of life.

If the cups are very big or deep, the subjects can be lazy and undisciplined, over-confident or tactless. They may hold on to emotional resentments. They may be indicating a need to be loved or an over-passionate nature.

The arcade

The arcade connection.

Like the garland, the arcade takes two movements, an up and a down. Instead of cups, the formation looks like bridges, and that is what they are – bridges between the subconscious and expressed thought. Whereas garland subjects are spontaneous, arcade subjects are much more thoughtful. They are pragmatic and careful. This is a good clue to a creative person, but more the gifted craftsman rather than the free-flowing fine artist. The arcade is used by musicians and architects. They like to think things out, see things through. Diplomats often use the arcade.

Turning to the negative, when the bridges reach up too high or are unduly long, the subject can be haughty and suspicious, or can tend to be manipulative.

The angle

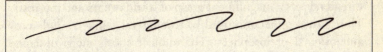

The angle connection.

This connection takes three movements of the pen, which makes it the most complicated and the most difficult to form freely and spontaneously. Subjects using this form of connection are firm and decisive. They like to exert careful control. There is a tremendous sense of duty and obligation. They are persistent and like to plan everything they do in great detail.

If the angle is extreme, made with heavy pressure or excessively jagged, then the subject could be domineering and somewhat lacking a sense of humour. They may well be unsociable. In very extreme cases they will show signs of irritability, and may be cruel or aggressive. The jagged angle may reveal a somewhat cold and ruthless person. It can also be a very good indicator of a lot of suppressed anger and violence. The shape of the angle and the way it is formed requires a great deal of control and determination, and these are exactly the character traits it reveals. Snow White's wicked stepmother would have been a heavy angular writer.

The thread

The thread connection.

Graphology

The thread connection is sometimes seen as a sub-group of the angle. However, it is very different, and extremely rare. The thread reveals a magnificent grasp of world events and interests. This is the connection used by true lateral thinkers, diplomats and original philosophers. The subject shows signs of being multi-talented, able to excel in whatever chosen career they go for; they have exceptional adaptability, being able to think on their feet quickly and instinctively.

They have to watch their health, though, as they can tire easily, and are prone to stress and can burn out before their time. If the thread ceases to be a connection and degenerates into a virtual straight line, the subject still has the sharp-brain agility, but is often unable to make good use of it. They become detached and cut off from reality. It is often seen in diplomats who have fallen from favour, or in university professors who have been overlooked in a promotion or funding conflict. It can indicate extreme stress or tiredness.

Uncial and cursive handwriting

We have dealt with the way letters are joined together into words.

But what about subjects who do not join their letters together? Their writing is called *uncial*. It means disconnected or broken, and is the opposite of *cursive* which means running or joined.

Uncial handwriting

Few people have their letters totally unconnected, most joining some letters but leaving a break in the middle of the word. These subjects are thoughtful, the break indicating almost a short pause while they gather their thoughts or stop for breath. They are observant and quick thinking, good at fine detail and usually talented.

> *hooted and the starlight on the sea which was*

Uncial handwriting.

The more letters that are uncial the more likely the subjects are to experience a sense of isolation, their thought processes breaking down under pressure. They may be insecure, troubled by inner fears and doubts. Uncial writing can be a sign of uncertainty or forgetfulness. It can often indicate loneliness.

Cursive handwriting

When the letters are all joined together, the writing is called cursive. This term also applies when the words themselves are joined together.

> *Class went and practice assignments. I am sure, however, with more effort to revise she could get a higher grade.*

Cursive handwriting.

Cursive handwriting is used by subjects who are sociable and outgoing. It is a sign of maturity and a well-balanced person who is enthusiastic about what they are writing about. You need to look at the overall letter formations and spacing, but the cursive style is usually adopted by subjects who have an easy-going approach to life and are sensible and reasoned.

If all the words are joined together, it can indicate an overactive mind or obsessional behaviour. If the cursive script is used erratically, occurring on some lines and not others, or used in some samples and not in others, it can indicate an indifference or neglectfulness or someone who does not think things through.

The word *cursive* and the word *cursory* share a common ancestry, and it is a useful way of remembering just what the cursive handwriting means: quick and hurried, and that is how subjects using the cursive style usually live their lives. If the cursive is regular and looks harmonious, it is a sign that they are quick and lively, but if it is irregular or intermittent, it is a sign of rushing or hastiness.

Legibility

When we write notes to ourselves, we often scribble them – we know what we are trying to say and the scribbled handwriting is a form of code that we can translate later. When we are writing for other people to read, we want to communicate, to get them to understand what we are trying to say. It is interesting to look at legibility from that point of view. Someone wants to communicate and then makes the message unreadable. It can reveal a lot about their attitude towards others.

Legible

If the message is to be read and understood, the writer will choose to make it so. They care that the reader will be able to make sense of their communication. Legible writing is a sign of sincerity and care. The writer takes the time and trouble to make sure the reader's task is not too difficult.

> Another thing — before you ...
> road I suddenly thought it might be the
> off the roundabout + not the 2nd. Did I go
> ... to add insult to injury?

Legible handwriting sample.

It is a patient and understanding approach. There should obviously be a balance, as in all things, between clarity and personality. If the handwriting shows no sign of originality, no style or novelty, but is just constructed with legibility as the only motive, then it can indicate an immaturity or lack of flamboyance. Extremely legible writing is often used by subjects whose letters predominantly occupy the middle zone. They can be expressing a solid heaviness about their thinking, perhaps a naivete or dull approach to life.

Illegible

Illegibility can be a sign of the inconsiderate. It can, however, also indicate a secretive side to someone's nature. We have to look at all the reasons why someone would write something, meant to be read by somebody else, and make it unreadable. It is an interesting area to look into.

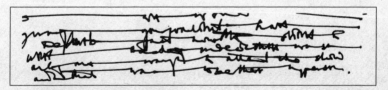

Illegible handwriting sample.

The reasons for illegibility can be thoughtlessness, lack of care, confusion and fear, poor manners, etc. But it can also indicate that the writer is fully aware that they are giving the reader extra work deciphering their writing. These writers feel sufficiently superior to us lesser folk for it not to matter; they are haughty, proud and arrogant, feeling it is beneath their dignity to write clearly for mere mortals.

Illegibility can also be a sign of anxiety. The writer is fearful of us reading what they have written in case we judge the content too harshly – they try to hide their feelings of inferiority behind a mask of illegibility.

Practice

- What are the four connections?
- What sort of connection would a diplomat probably use?
- What is uncial handwriting? What does it indicate?
- What is cursive handwriting? What does it indicate?

8

letters and numbers

Now we have covered the basics, it is time to start looking at the detail. Once we have arrived at an initial appraisal of a subject's handwriting, we might need confirmation of some salient point. This is where the individual letters can help. If you had the time and patience you could keep a record of how each subject forms each letter of the alphabet. It is probably not necessary at this stage, but it can be helpful to have a knowledge of some of the more important letter formations. I will leave the 't' and the 'i' for a separate chapter, as they are really a considerable area of study and deserve separate attention, and we have already dealt with the 'w' and the 'd'.

Letters

We are taught at school how to form the letters, and there is

Graphology

obviously an influence that will always remain with us. How far away from that influence we stray can be a good indication of how independent, rebellious or creative we are. Look at the individual letters. Do they subscribe to some textbook form? Or are they unique, flamboyant, unusual, simplistic? Each different style will tell us something different about the writer. The letter formations will usually reflect how the writer likes to live their life.

> which I enclose a cheque for
> am walking around as if I have a broom

Simplistic and elaborated samples.

We can now begin to look at a few of the traits revealed by *simplistic* and *elaborated* letter formations.

Simplistic letters

Straightforward people.
Positive: Mature, intelligent, practical, ordered, direct, observant, able to concentrate, able to attend to essentials, economical, objective, cultured, thoughtful, careful.
Negative: Tactless, neglectful, insincere, cold, ruthless, no sense of style or beauty, few interests, no feeling for history or tradition, no social interests, reserved, dull.

Elaborated letters

Complex people.
Positive: Original, creative, traditional, interested, tasteful, friendly, cultured, sense of form and beauty.

Negative: Vain, pompous, lacking refinement, vulgar, eccentric, need to be approved of, need to show off, affectation, boastful, very formal, unclear thinking, confused.

Major traits of letter groups

The groups of letters we are going to look at now are for confirmations if you need some additional material to support an interpretation. You need only look at the lower case letters (the little ones, not the capitals). Look for letters that stand out as larger or smaller than the other letters around them. Look for ones that are stunted or flamboyant.

a, e, o

These three letters form an interesting group where we can look for signs of jealousy and honesty among other traits. We can regard these letters as identical for the purposes of this exercise.

1 *e o*   *Elliptic*: subject prone to anxiety.

2 *a o*   *Closed*: dependable, diplomatic.

3 *a o*   *Open at the top*: outspoken.

4 *a o*   *Open at the bottom*: dishonest.

5 *a o*   *Open wide*: gossipy.

6 *aue*   *Large*: jealousy.

7 *a*   *Looped at the top*: secretive.

8   *Double looped*: deceitful, secretive, convincing liar.

9   *Greek or Celtic 'e'*: educated, creative, intelligent.

b

10 *able*   *Small*: someone not interested in imaginative ideas.

11 *abee*   *Large*: imaginative, fanciful.

12   *Looped*: can feel unloved.

13   *No loop*: individualistic, independent.

14   *Open*: intuitive.

c, s, u, v

15   *Square*: calculating, persistent.

16   *Varies*: versatile, could be unreliable.

17   *Heavy beginning or ink dot*: guilty secrets.

18   *Squiggly*: sense of humour.

19 *See above*   *Large*: excitable.

20 *see above*   *Small*: lacking in self-confidence.

f, k

21	*f k*	*Knotted:* resilient, strong, forceful.
22	*f k*	*Far right and curling forward:* altruistic, caring.
23	*f k*	*Short second stroke:* ambitious.
24	*f k*	*Long second stroke:* charmer, lounge lizard.
25	*for peek*	*Enlarged:* petty, worries over trivia.
26	*for peek*	*Small:* lacking in confidence.
27	*for peek*	*Tall:* enterprising.

g, j, p, q, y

28	*g j p y*	*Elliptic loop:* anxiety.
29	*g j p y*	*Arcaded bottom to left with no loop:* avoids responsibility.
30	*g j p y*	*Angular or pointed bottom to left with no loop:* domineering (especially at home).
31	*g j p y*	*Big rounded loop:* passionate, sexual.
32	*g j p y*	*Straight loop, average length:* realistic, reliable, pragmatic.

Graphology

33 *Short stem, no loop:* cold, indifferent, unresponsive.

34 *Stunted or heavy pressure stem:* sexual worries or problems.

35 *Triangular loop:* stubborn, obstinate.

36 *Big triangular loops:* frustration, experiencing setbacks.

37 *Open loop to left:* romantic, immature.

38 *Curly stem but not looped:* not in touch with reality, dreamer, unrealistic, given to fantasy.

39 *Long pointed loops:* critical, acidic.

40 *Small ticks to the right, no loop:* aggressive, irritable, enterprising.

41 *Long stem, closed loop like an 'o':* needs security.

42 *Long stem, no loop:* likes freedom, restless.

h, n

43 *Angular:* aggressive.

44 *Very rounded:* needing love.

45 *he Needs* — *Tall*: needing attention and/or approval.

46 *she needs* — *Short*: lacking initiative and confidence.

47 *b n* — *Very ornate*: self-satisfaction.

m, w

48 *M* — *m: Second point exaggerated*: needs approval.

49 *W* — *w: Second point high*: independent.

50 *M* — *m: Last stroke descending below baseline*: arrogance.

51 *W* — *w: Last stroke rising up into upper zone*: literary, imaginative.

r

52 *are* — *Short following stroke*: ambitious.

53 *are* — *Enlarged*: ruthless in business.

x

54 *x* — *Doubled*: will never give up.

55 *x* — *Curly*: powerful sense of own identity.

Graphology

z

56 **Z** *Straight, no loop:* pragmatic, intolerant.

57 **ʒ** *Curly, looped:* flamboyant, creative, time-waster.

Numbers

Sometimes you may be called upon to make an analysis of someone's writing and only be able to get hold of a list of numbers or some calculation they may have done. So it is important to know that the numbers can be interpreted in pretty much the same way as the letters.

Are they simplistic or elaborated? Neat or scruffy? Legible or not?

Notice very closed numbers like the 4. This can be a very secretive person. An open 4 indicates a much more open subject. The same goes for most of the numbers.

Look out for the crossed 7. They may be European, trained as an accountant, or have a desire to draw attention to themselves.

Very square numbers can indicate a mental confusion or someone trying to cover their mathematical bewilderment.

So we have now looked at letters and numbers. Have we missed anything? After the practice questions it will be time for the 't' and the 'i'.

Practice

- What is meant by simplistic and elaborate letter formations?
- What do they indicate, both positive and negative?
- Where would we look for signs of jealousy and honesty?
- What would a Greek 'e' indicate?
- What do stunted or heavy pressure stems reveal?
- What does an enlarged 'r' reveal about someone's business skills?

9

dotting and crossing

In personnel selection, more attention is probably given to the 'i' and the 't' than any other letters. This is because the 'i' and the 't' give us valuable clues as to how people see themselves in the work-place, and how they fit in with others, even their leadership qualities.

When someone is selecting an applicant for a position, it is essential that they get the right person. Mistakes can be very costly, and personnel selectors will use any tool to enable them to get it right. Graphology is just such a valuable tool.

Positioning of the 'i' dot

This is where we look if we want to find out how a potential candidate works alone. If left unsupervised, will they take advantage of the situation? Are they trustworthy and industrious? Do they need constant support? Are they able to concentrate? All this information is helpful to the personnel selector.

There are so many different types and styles of 'i's that it is impossible to cover them all. However, I shall give you the main ones and I hope that having picked up the way graphology works, you should be able to assess any others you may come across in your future projects.

Remember though that the 'i', as any other single factor, must not be read alone. You have to take a lot of factors into consideration before giving an analysis of a subject's character. No single factor will give you enough information to jump to a conclusion. You can jump when you have analysed every single aspect you possibly can, not before.

Left slant

1. *Left slant, dot overhead average*: good memory, cautious.
2. *Left slant, dot overhead low*: cautious, feels restrained.
3. *Left slant, dot overhead high*: accuracy, inquiring mind.
4. *Left slant, left dot average*: cautious and practical.
5. *Left slant, left dot low*: extremely cautious, hesitant.
6. *Left slant, left dot high*: prying, inquisitive.
7. *Left slant, right dot average*: good planning abilities.
8. *Left slant, right dot low*: practical, cautious but active.
9. *Left slant, right dot high*: good surveying abilities.

Graphology

Upright

10 *Upright, left dot average*: practical, realistic but cautious.
11 *Upright, left dot low*: industrious but needs to be told what to do.
12 *Upright, left dot high*: holding back, not satisfied.
13 *Upright, dot overhead average*: accurate, decisive.
14 *Upright, dot overhead low*: needs motivating.
15 *Upright, dot overhead high*: may need enthusiasm curbing.
16 *Upright, right dot average*: active, likes new projects.
17 *Upright, right dot low*: practical, realistic.
18 *Upright, right dot high*: excellent at planning, keen.

Right slant

19 *Right slant, left dot average*: realistic, cautious.
20 *Right slant, left dot low*: finds problems where there are none.
21 *Right slant, left dot high*: detached, aloof.
22 *Right slant, dot overhead average*: accurate, balanced, positive.
23 *Right slant, dot overhead low*: losing enthusiasm.

24	ट	*Right slant, dot overhead high*: ambitious, could be impulsive.
25	ट	*Right slant, right dot average*: intuitive, intelligent.
26	ट	*Right slant, right dot low*: impatient, restless.
27	ट	*Right slant, right dot high*: visionary, enterprising, daring.

Distinctive

28	ι	*Left placed arc*: observant, cautious.
29	ι	*Right placed arc*: watchful, quiet.
30	ι	*Convex*: deceitful, untrustworthy.
31	ι	*Slanted dot*: hasty, lively.
32	ι	*No dot*: careless, indolent.
33	ι	*Circled dot*: creative, individualistic, attention seeking.
34	ι	*Lined dot*: critical.
35	ι	*Squiggle*: sense of humour.
36	ι	*Tented dot*: meddlesome, derogatory.
37	ιy	*Joined dot (to next letter)*: mature, decisive, quick thinking.
38	ι	*Dot on the stem*: boredom, restlessness, carelessness.

Graphology

Now to run through your samples and check the 'i' dot positions. How do they relate to what you already know about your friends?

Time for 't's

If the 'i' tells us how people work alone, then the 't' tells us how they relate to others, and especially their leadership qualities. The 't' bar indicates how much control they like, or are prepared to exercise, over other employees. But remember it cannot be taken in isolation. It is an important factor but you must confirm your analysis from other components in the handwriting.

Whereas we take the lower case 'i', it is relevant to take both the upper and lower case 't' (capitals and little letters). The upper case 't' is used a lot and can be the most revealing of letters. It is one we form often and do not think about much. It therefore becomes habitual, exposing unconscious traits that might otherwise be hidden.

And again, like the 'i', there are probably as many variations of the 't' as there are writers. We shall deal with the main ones.

Left 'T' bar

1　　　　　　　　　　*Low*: lack of motivation.

2　　　　　　　　　　*Medium*: cautious, hesitant.

3　　　　　　　　　　*High*: reluctant to lead.

Crossed 'T' bar

4　　　　　　　　　　*Low*: lacks self-confidence.

5　　　　　　　　　　*Medium*: attention to detail.

Dotting and Crossing

6 **t**   *High*: desire to control.

Right 'T' bar

7 **t**   *Low, short*: reluctant to take responsibility.

8 **t**   *High, short*: open-minded, limited, considerate.

9 **t**   *Low, long*: can solve problems, diplomatic.

10 **t**   *Medium, long*: accepts responsibility.

11 **t**   *High long*: leadership potential, responsible.

Right 'T' bar, detached

12 **t**   *Low, medium*: enterprising, accepts challenges.

13 **t**   *Medium, medium*: needs to control, impatient, goal orientated.

14 **t**   *High, medium*: real leadership qualities.

Right 'T' bar, detached, upward

15 **t t**   *Low*: likes to control.

16 **t t**   *Medium*: ambitious, leadership material, can be difficult to get on with.

17 **t t**   *High*: natural leaders, highly intelligent, executive abilities.

Graphology

As can be seen from the above list there are hundreds of combinations. I have only listed the ones for the upright 't's. You could consider such formations as: a left-slanted 't' with detached upward bar with right placement; or a right-slanted 't' with detached left bar sloping upwards.

The permutations are endless. Remember, as a general rule:

- Left slant: caution.
- Upright: balance.
- Right slant: enthusiasm.
- Low 't' bar: holding back.
- Medium 't' bar: responsible.
- High 't' bar: control, leadership.
- Upward 't' bar: dynamic, motivated, ambitious.
- Straight 't' bar: confident, practical.
- Downward 't' bar: losing interest, despondency.

Some more 'T's

18   'T' bar above upright: bossy, ambitious.

19   'T' bar above, high: unrealistic dreamer.

20   Very long 't' bar to right: protective or patronizing.

21   Looped: proud.

22   Connected: quick thinking, logical.

23   Tight loop: stubborn, determined.

24   Dot added: aggression.

25 　*Looped and barred*: vain.

26 　*Wavy 't' bar*: sense of humour, frivolous.

27 　*No 't' bar*: careless, will not accept responsibility.

28 　*Looped and curling downward*: feeling of talents being ignored, resentful, sulky.

29 　*Tiny 't' bar*: repressed, lacks confidence.

So there you have it, 60 variations (including capitals and lower case) of the 't's and 't' bars and enough clues to be able to decipher any others you may encounter.

Before you go on to learn about signatures, test yourself on the practice questions for this chapter. There has been a lot to remember!

Practice

- What does the 'i' reveal?
- Would you trust your business to someone who joins their dots to the next letter?
- What does the 't' reveal?
- How many variations of the 't' bar are there? (trick question)
- Why do personnel selectors look to the 'i' and 't' so much?
- What does a low left 't' bar indicate?
- What does a right bar, detached, upward, high, reveal?

10

signing off

As we have moved away from being primitive people into an increasingly structured society, we have needed to invent symbols to replace our basic human behaviour. It is no longer acceptable to beat our chest in a gesture of aggression or power; but we can use an enlarged signature to demonstrate our strength. We would be considered odd if we lowered our head in a submissive gesture when we feel intimidated; but we can use a tiny signature when we feel like that.

Our signature tells the world how we would like to be viewed. If you know the basics of signature identification, it can be a considerable advantage before you have even met the writer. You can already know what motivates them, how they are likely to present themselves, and probably how they will need to be handled.

What does your signature reveal?

In this age of computers and word processors, the signature may be the only evidence of a personal style available to us. That is why many personnel selectors insist that you fill in employment applications in handwriting. They know how essential that information will be to them.

But if you only have the signature to go on, it can still give you a very valuable insight into a person's character.

In the modern world, the signature of a person is the evidence that they exist. Take your credit card for example. The signature on it is you. It is considered to be so permanently you as to be good enough to identify you. It is taken for granted that it does not change and remains constant enough to be acceptable over a number of years. It is unique.

The people in the bank may well recognize you, but they will still insist that you sign your cheque on the back to prove that it is really you. In fact your signature, in many circumstances, would probably be more acceptable than you in person. Forgers know this and use it to their own advantage.

Another example is your passport. You have your photograph taken and it is pasted on to your passport, which usually lasts for ten years. During which time you have lost or gained weight; aged; changed your hair style or colour; grown taller or shrunk; taken to wearing glasses; given up glasses in favour of contact lenses; grown a beard or shaved one off; had your hair permed or waved or plaited; had your nose done; gone bald; lost your teeth or had them capped; and added to the lines and wrinkles in no uncertain manner. And they still expect to recognize you at Customs. But your signature will not have changed.

And if it has, I bet it has not changed that much, maybe a slight tweak here and there to reflect a major life change, such as getting married. Do not forget, if a recently married woman adopts her new husband's surname, she will change her entire

Graphology

signature. Try to get 'before' and 'after' samples.

So, your signature is you. It is accepted as such on your driving licence, credit cards, passport, personal ID, library ticket, medical card, national insurance card, household bills, cheques, court documents, marriage licence, job applications. The list is endless.

Your signature is so much you that it even survives your death. It is still you on your will, telling the world what you want from beyond the grave.

Are you now convinced of just how important your signature is? And most people give it little thought. They just make one up when they are quite young and then are stuck with it for the rest of their life, and beyond that.

It is even our history. You can see early influences in a person's life in their signature because it is formed when they are so young. It is the original and unchanging symbol of our own existence.

It is probably also the only part of our handwriting that we voluntarily practise when we are young. Some people spend a considerable amount of time getting it just right: it has to look right; reflect how we want the world to see us; appear grown-up and sophisticated; express our individualism or our plainness. Check your own if you have samples from your childhood, teenage years or early twenties. Does it vary much? Can you see the progression as you have matured?

So what does it all mean? This is where we will begin to analyse individual types of signature in detail.

Signature same as handwriting

If the signature has the same overall features as the rest of the handwriting, the subject is natural, uncomplicated and objective. Their writing reveals how they want the world to see them. You will probably have reached a fairly detailed assessment of their character already. The signature, being the same, will verify your assessment.

Signature different from handwriting

Rising or falling signatures indicate optimism or pessimism. If there is a difference, as in a rising signature with the general handwriting having an overall falling appearance, then the subject is putting on a brave face. They are still in there, slugging away.

If the signature is falling with a general rising script, then the subject's optimism is taking a downward turn; they may be suffering temporary setbacks. You need to see a few samples written over a period of time to see if it's a trend or a permanent decline.

Larger than writing

The subject is self-reliant, independent, ambitious, wants to be seen and recognized, wants to stand out, possibly feels repressed in their life and is capable of being more flamboyant.

Larger signature.

Graphology

Much larger than writing

This type of signature is used by subjects who are proud, possibly without cause. They can be pretentious show-offs who like to be flamboyant and extreme in their behaviour.

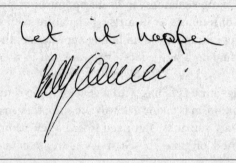

Much larger signature.

Smaller than writing

The subject feels humble, doesn't want to draw attention to themselves, suffers from feelings of inferiority, has taken on too much and feels they can't cope.

Smaller signature.

Much smaller than writing

Can indicate extreme feelings of anxiety, depression, emotional problems. They can be unable to relate to the outside world, trying to make themselves so small that they will not be noticed.

Much smaller signature.

Left slanted signature, right slanted writing

This is quite a rare combination. It indicates a certain reserve or conflict. The subject is not really as enthusiastic as they would have us believe. They are sensitive souls and easily hurt. Treat them gently, it is hard work for them to be as lively as they seem, it is all an act.

Left slanted signature, right slanted writing.

Graphology

Right slanted signature, left slanted writing

These subjects are clever and careful. They are naturally secretive. They like you to think they are spontaneous and lively, but in reality they are much more manipulative. Be wary of trusting these subjects as they are masking their true identities.

Right slanted signature, left slanted writing.

Signature with flourishes

Can be used by subjects with a real need to be noticed. They can be ostentatious, possibly vain and flamboyant. They are the eccentrics, the actors of the world, bright and colourful. Compare how the signature fits in with the general handwriting. Is it similar? Very different? You should know by now what each would mean.

Signature with flourishes.

Signature with lasso

This is a very self-assertive signature. The subject likes to be in control. They would resent any interference in their private life. They can be fiercely independent, almost to the point of obsessional behaviour.

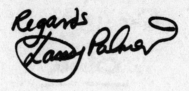

Signature with lasso

Encircled signature

This can indicate a lack of self-confidence or of someone being in a situation in which they feel uncomfortable or stressed. The circle is a feature that can suddenly appear and just as suddenly disappear; check the subject's personal relationships. It may well be a sign of incompatibility. It can also indicate suppressed anger.

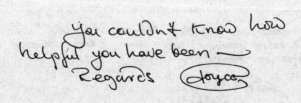

Encircled signature.

Graphology

Underlined signature

Subjects using this type of signature like to take responsibility, both for themselves and for others. They have a justifiable sense of importance. They are firm and determined. You cannot fool them, they know what is what.

Underlined signature.

Illegible signature

The signature of subjects who like their true nature to be concealed. You have to look elsewhere in their writing to find out what it is that they are trying to hide. It may be that they feel out of their depth, or it could be an emotional coldness. This applies if the rest of their writing is legible. If both the signature and the handwriting are illegible, it may be a sign of great intellect.

Illegible signature.

Placements

Where the writers chose to place their signature on the page can also be very revealing. It is not only what they are trying to tell us, but also the manner in which they are doing the telling.

Right placement

Enthusiastic and lively. They face the future with optimism and hope. They are excited by new projects and greet each new day with enthusiasm.

```
                Yours sincerely

                        [signature]

                Adrian Talpa
```

Right placement.

Extreme right placement

The enthusiasm shown in the right placement is being replaced with a wild excitement. They are not only excited by the future, but also cannot wait to get into it. They can be manic and bouncy, and exhausting to be around for too long. Again, check the rest of the handwriting for confirmation, but it looks like you have another 'Tigger' on your hands.

Graphology

Extreme right placement.

Centre placement

They are showing a need for security and can be indecisive. You would think a centre placement would indicate a well-balanced subject, but you need to see other indicators in the handwriting to confirm this assessment.

Centre placement.

Left placement

These subjects are shy and do not like to push themselves forward too much. They do know what they are doing, however, and do it well; it is just that they do not like to take the credit. They are unassuming, and do not like to show off. They can be telling the world that they like peace and quiet, so do not invite them to too many wild parties as you will only frighten them.

> I am very grateful and will write again later.
>
> Yours faithfully
>
> *Edna Welthope (mrs).*
>
> Edna Welthorpe (Mrs)

Left placement.

Extreme left placement

These subjects are so shy or retiring that it has developed into anxiety and depression. This signature can sometimes indicate agoraphobia. They don't like to go out into the world at all.

> **Regards and best wishes**
>
> *Martin Phelps.*
>
> **Mr. M. Phelps**

Extreme left placement.

Forenames and surnames

Does your subject use their forename, surname or both? Or just their initials? They all mean different things.

The forename is the subject's private life. This is how they are at home, in their place of love and security. It indicates how they feel when they are alone or with their family.

The surname is the subject's public life. This is them at work, socializing and being out in the world.

If the forename is more showy, bigger or more clearly written, it indicates that their private life is where the subject feels happier. They like being at home. They are not one of the world's great gogetters, preferring to live a quiet life. They are usually warm, soft subjects who are loving and kind.

If they only use the forename, then they may well have retired completely from public life, either physically or emotionally.

If the surname is the big one, more showy or embellished, then being in the limelight is where the writer feels happiest. Out in the world is where they can relax. They like to get the job done, and be on to the next one. They are enterprising and resourceful; they like to be seen and can socialize well.

If the surname becomes too large or too flamboyant, at the expense of the forename, then the subject can be attracted to the sort of wild parties I warned you not to invite the left-placed signature users to.

If both forename and surname are pretty much the same size, you have a subject who is well balanced and at ease both at home and out in the world. Check the placement though – it may indicate something different.

If the forename and surname have the same sort of formation, they could vary in slant. The traits indicated depend on which way the slant goes. It indicates a conflict between private and public life.

Letters from friends will usually just have their forenames, so you need to get hold of a business letter (or sneak a peep at their credit card) to see what their true signature is like. Friends that sign their personal letters with their full signature are unable to relax.

So what about people who have two signatures? These are quite rare. It indicates that they lead two separate lives.

There may well be a formal business life and a wild social side. Or it may be that there is something unsavoury being hidden.

Practice

- What can the signature tell us about a person?
- Does your signature change?
- What does it reveal if the signature is much larger than the handwriting?
- Would you trust someone who underlined their signature?
- What does it reveal if the signature is placed to the left?
- Is it common for someone to have two signatures? And what would it tell us about the person if they did?

11

odds and ends

We have now covered all the main aspects of graphology, but there are still a few more features of a person's handwriting which can be very revealing.

The capital 'I'
If the signature reveals how the writer likes the world to see them, then the capital 'I' (used as a personal pronoun) reveals how they feel about themselves. If the signature is the *ego* (the conscious), then the capital 'I' is the *id* (the subconscious). This is where we look if we want to see the inner fears, the insecurities, the dark hidden stuff that we all love to know.

The first sign to check for is size. Look at the examples of capital 'I's on page 89 and then compare them with the list below.

Odds and Ends

1 If it is larger than the rest of the surrounding letters, it indicates a powerful sense of self-importance.
2 Smaller and it is indicating a feeling of inferiority.

Then look at the slant.

3 To the left (while the rest of the writing is straight or right slanting) it indicates an inner anxiety, a fear of pushing themselves forward.
4 To the right (while the rest slants to the left or is straight), it may indicate someone living under an oppressive regime; they are actually more optimistic than they are being allowed to be.

Now look at the way it is formed. Is it a genuine capital? Or merely an enlarged lower case 'i'?

5 The true capital indicates someone confident and at ease with themselves.
6 A dotted lower case 'i' is a sign of someone struggling to make it in in the world and feeling unsure of their worthiness. It may well change to a capital 'I' if, and when, they have achieved success.
7 A high looped 'I' coming from the left and looping to the right at the bottom indicates someone hanging on to the past, unable to move enthusiastically into their future. They may well have experienced intense sadness in their past, lost a dear loved one, and have not come to terms with their grief.
8 A capital 'I' with the top bar above the stem indicates an unrealistic view of themselves. Perhaps, as a result of their inflated ideas of their own talents or success, they may well like to talk about themselves a lot.

Graphology

Now look at spacing.

9 If the 'I' is placed close to the word following it, the subject likes company and is sociable and friendly.
10 Too close, and they may well be clingy or emotionally immature.
11 If the 'I' is placed close to the word preceding it, then the subject may well look to the past for their happier times.
12 Too close and they may well hang on to past resentments and find it hard to forgive.
13 Equally spaced between the following and preceding words, and the subject is well adjusted and feels at ease with themselves.
14 A flourished or embellished 'I' can be a sign that the subject feels superior to others around them. As always, check other facets of the handwriting.

I think you should now know enough about how graphology works not to need each and every example of the many forms of 'I's. It's time for you to start doing some work on your own. Identify the following and match them to the descriptions already given.

Practice

Examples of capital 'I's.

Envelopes

Like margins, envelopes can give a first impression that can influence how we see the writer. If the signature reveals how the subject wants to be seen, then the address on the envelope is a good indication of their attitude to the outside world. It will also reveal their caring side. Do they care? Are they indifferent? The envelope may not tell you more than you already know, but it might.

The address on the envelope will often be handwritten, while the letter inside may have been typed. Apart from the signature, it could be the only sample you can get hold of. Look at the samples on page 90 and compare them with the notes on page 91.

Graphology

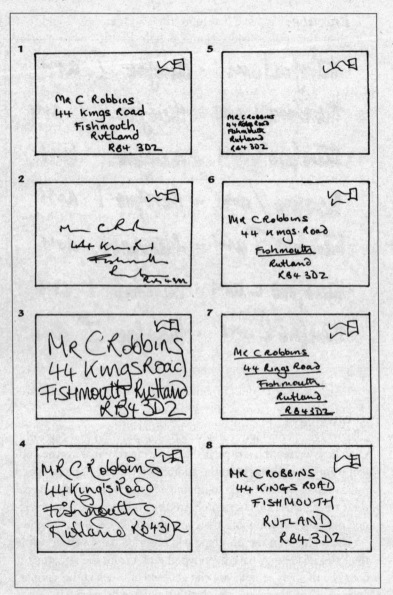

Examples of envelopes.

1. Legible: it may have had more time and attention paid to it than the letter inside. Some people like to make a good impression.
2. Illegible: lack of consideration and superiority. Who cares what a mere post office worker thinks, or if it increases the effort they have to make to decipher the address?
3. Larger writing than the letter contains: more assertive than you would think.
4. Larger, flourished: ostentatious display, boastful, bragging.
5. Smaller writing than the letter contains: not very assertive.
6. The city underlined: knows what is important.
7. Everything underlined: unable to separate importance from trivia.
8. All capitals: immaturity, lack of imagination.

Address placement

Again, look at the examples given on page 92 and compare them with the interpretations below.

9. *Left*: cannot make friends.
10. *Right*: over-dependent on other people for emotional security.
11. *Top*: detached from reality, pompous.
12. *Bottom*: over-dependency on material things, pleasure loving. *Centred*: well balanced, rational, caring, thoughtful.

Think about all the different combinations and use the chart on page 92 to make an exact analysis, for example, top left: drives people away with their pompous attitude. Bottom right: expects you to pick up the bill in restaurants.

So, we have looked at every aspect and you should now have a basic grounding in graphology. It is time to put it all together.

Graphology

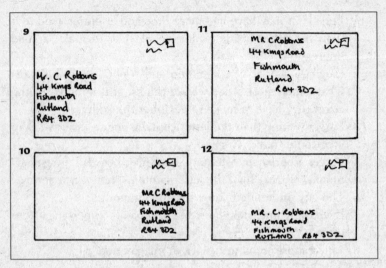

Examples of address placements.

Top left	Top centre	Top right
Centre left	Centre	Centre right
Bottom left	Bottom centre	Bottom right

The nine envelope placements.

12

making an analysis

Although most graphologists do not work to a set pattern, some do. Those who do not like to, treat each sample as unique. It keeps their work fresh and they maintain a healthy interest in each new project.

Suggested procedures

As you are beginning it might to helpful for you to follow a set procedure at this stage. You can abandon it as soon as you feel confident enough to go it alone. If your interpretations suffer as a result of abandoning the procedure, you can always return to it. And it is only a guide. Some samples will deserve a different treatment, if only because some quirkiness stands out and warrants being dealt with out of turn.

It is all a question of balance. Sometimes a sample will, on first glance, reveal little that stands out. In this instance, having a logical procedure to follow can be useful.

There are two ways of approaching the operation. We can look for graphological characteristics first and match them with character traits. Or we can do it the other way round; have a check list of traits and look for the formations that would indicate them.

I will give you both methods and you can use the one that suits you best.

Looking for graphological traits

It is probably best to start at the beginning and work through to the end in much the same way that this book has been laid out, so, use a checklist, something like the one below.

General impression: special characteristics, what stands out?
Paper
Ink
Style
Margins
Content
Pressure
Pen
Legibility
Regularity/size:
Check letters
Words
Overall affect
Slants:
Letters
Lines

> ***Dominant traits:***
> Loops
> Stems
> The 'w'
> The 'd'
> ***Space:***
> Between words
> Between lines
> ***Widths:***
> Words
> Lines
> ***Starting***
> ***Terminals***
> ***Connections:***
> Garland/arcade/angle/thread
> Cursive/uncial
> ***Fullness/leanness***
> ***Right/left tendencies***
> ***The 'i' dots***
> ***'T' bars***
> ***Capital 'I'***
> ***Signature***

You may even like to award points for each feature or some other system of keeping track. Perhaps a coded system designed only for you.

Looking for character traits

You may like to examine the sample for character traits first and match them with the formations.

Graphology

You could begin by looking for:

- How we relate to ourselves.

- How we relate to others.

- What we think of ourselves.

- What we think of others.

- How we work alone.

- How we work with others.

- Our leadership qualities.

- Introvert/extrovert.

- Optimistic/pessimistic.

- Happy/depressed.

- Calm/excited.

Both methods work. It is up to you which you use. Or you can work out your own method based on a combination of the two. Or use none at all and just intuitively feel your way through each sample.

I must stress at this point that you are dealing with a very sensitive area and confidentiality must be of the utmost importance. Keep your files locked away. Keep your records in such a manner that only you will be able to understand them. And keep your samples private. You will lose your subject's respect, and seriously jeopardize your own reputation, if you do not take these precautions.

Making an Analysis

On the following pages are some samples. I want you to assess them in whatever manner you decide. After each sample, I have given an appraisal. These appraisals are approved by the subjects who submitted the samples as being accurate. See how close you get.

After that there are some useful addresses and some suggested further reading if you would like to take the wonderful and rewarding subject of graphology further.

Author's signature.

13

samples for practice

On the next pages are a few samples for you to study in detail. Go through them following the instructions given in this book, and see what you come up with. I will then analyse them step-by-step so that you can see where I get the information from. Then there are two without my analysis, but with an interpretation. See how close to mine you get (without looking first). And finally there are two samples for you to practise on. You can ignore them if you have obtained samples of your own by now.

The samples

We begin with samples donated by two sisters. This is an interesting way to carry out an analysis because, at first glance, they look very similar. There are, however, sufficient differences to be able to accurately assess both individual characters, and they are quite different. Study them before you turn to the analysis.

They are marked A and B. The information you need is:
A: female, aged 32, left-handed, British.
B: female, aged 29, right-handed, British.

They had the same upbringing, attended the same school (even had the same teachers), and were asked to write a letter saying the same thing as each other to help you spot differences.

> 23, High Street
> Kingston
> Surrey
>
> Dear Richard
>
> As requested here is a sample of my handwriting. I think it is an interesting exercise to compare my writing with that of my sister.
>
> It will be quite exciting to be included in a book on graphology. Will we be famous?
>
> Good luck with this, and all your future projects.
>
> Love & love,
>
> Rosie.
> xx

Sample A.

Graphology

> 135A Penguin St.
> London
>
> Dear Richard,
>
>   As requested here is a sample of my handwriting. I think it is an interesting exercise to compare my writing with that of my sister. It'll be quite exciting to be included in a book on graphology, will we be famous? Good luck with this & all your future projects.
>
>   Masses of love
>   Katie
>   xxx

Sample B.

The interpretations

So, how did you get on? Let us begin with the overall appearance.

Appearance: both samples are neat, well spaced and have a pleasing, balanced appearance. A has a slightly closer left margin and uses three distinct paragraphs. B's right margin runs on more and does not use any paragraphs. What does this tell you? A is a little more organized? B is a little more spontaneous? Yes.

Zones: A uses the upper zone more. B uses the lower zone more. What does that tell you? A is more drawn to intellectual pursuits while B is more of an instinctive doer.

Width of words: A's words are wider (measure the words 'graphology' and 'handwriting' to see the difference) than B's, indicating she worries less and is more happy-go-lucky.

Space between words: B is wider, indicating she is not as confident in herself as A.

Spacing between lines: A uses a narrower spacing than B, indicating she is more conscious of needing people around. A's loops and stems overlap, indicating she acts more on her feelings.

The 'w': both are slightly turned inward indicating introversion. Confirm this by checking the 'd's.

The 'd': B's is upright and the introversion very mild. A's, however, does follow the 'w' by turning inward as well (see the 'd' of 'Richard'), indicating she is more introvert than her sister. A's 'd's are also looped (see last 'd' of 'included'), which may indicate that A is vainer than B.

Loops: neither uses much in the way of loops, indicating they are both pragmatic.

Stems: A's are medium while B's are longer (see the 'y' in 'graphology'). It could make her stronger and more romantic and idealistic than her sister.

Slants: both are upright. Both are independent and reliable.

Slopes: both are horizontal and so both stable.

Connections: B uses the garland, which makes her open and honest. A uses the angle, and so she is firm and decisive.

Both use cursive script: a sign of maturity and that they are well-balanced. They are easy going but sensible.

Legibility: B's is slightly more legible than A's, which tends to overlap the lines below (look at the word 'sample'). This indicates that B is more considerate, or it might be that A is more intellectual.

Some letter differences: both use the Greek 'e', but A's turns more upward. The Greek 'e' indicates intelligence, creativity and a good education. The upward turn on A's indicates that she is more likely to use her mind in her work.

Compare the 'k's and the 'r's: B's are medium while A's are longer and more ornate (look at the 'k' in 'book' and the capital 'R' in Richard). This would make her a tough negotiator in business, but with considerable charm.

The loops of 'g/j/p/q/y': A's are closed while B's are open. They are both big and healthy. A is passionate while her sister is more romantic. B's are also longer, indicating a need for more freedom.

Both 'x's are almost doubled: both sisters are persistent.

The dotted 'i's: A's are upright/left dot/medium; she is practical and realistic but cautious. B's are upright/right dot/medium; she is active and likes new projects.

The 't'-bar: A's are crossed/medium/right long; she is protective and pays attention to detail. B's are crossed/medium/right upward; she is enthusiastic and pays attention to detail.

The capital 'I': both are upright, well spaced and plain; they are well adjusted and feel at ease with themselves.

Signature: A's is upward/larger/underlined/slight left placement/flourished; she has inner optimism, is self-reliant, takes responsibility, is unassuming, and her inner self is more flamboyant than she reveals to the outside world. B's is horizontal/same size as writing/slight right placement; she is balanced, natural, objective, uncomplicated and lively. Also notice the more flamboyant 'K' in 'B's signature. What does this tell us? That she would like to be more outward in her business, more ruthless?

So, what do we have? If you go through and collect all the traits from each sample, you should be able now to put them together into a character analysis.

Samples for Practice

A: Organized. Intellectual. Self-confident. Sociable. In touch with her feelings. Slightly introvert. Cares about her appearance. Pragmatic. Independent. Reliable. Stable. Firm. Decisive. Mature. Well balanced. Creative. Tough negotiator. Charming. Passionate. Persistent. Practical. Self-reliant. Takes responsibility. Could be more spontaneous. Could relinquish some control.

B: Spontaneous. Active. Pragmatic. Romantic. Idealistic. Independent. Reliable. Stable. Open. Honest. Mature. Well balanced. Considerate. Creative. Persistent. Likes freedom. Likes new projects. Enthusiastic. Lively. Could be more motivated, more serious about her career.

So how accurate are we?

A is a successful professional writer. She is an independent freelance business journalist. Intelligent and creative, she enjoys working on her own and likes the intellectual challenge her work gives her. She can be inclined to be too serious and can be bossy.

B is a freelance make-up artist. She is romantic and idealistic, and enjoys socializing and travels more than her sister. She has a lively personality, and adjusts quickly to new situations. She agrees she could be more ambitious.

Both sisters have verified the analyses as being accurate.

Graphology

Aubrey has been quieter since March.
We have missed his looming sense of
wonder. How could it be that the other
characters in this awesome motel have
said nothing of the disappearance?
The gardens are still now at night,
there is the scent of foxgloves, the
wilder delights of the Edwardian Houseboats.
Candles gutter in the east wing, her
lips curl across the page as I write.
"Then you cannot find it in your
heart to forgive?"
"Forgive? Forgive? How could they
expect this of me?"

Paul Selby.

Sample 1. Information: male, aged 45, right-handed British.

Sample 1

Creative. Optimistic. Eccentric. Lively. Inclined to get despondent. Energy reserves erratic. Proud. Achiever. Good planning abilities. Extrovert. Enterprising. Very forceful. Very strong character. Likes freedom. Likes travel. Dynamic. Motivated. Determined. Quick thinking. Logical. Creative. Fiercely independent. Intelligent.

So how did you get on?

Sample 1 is a college lecturer of English, media communications and film. He is a very creative, artistic person who spends long periods travelling. He could be styled 'larger than life'. A dynamic character. I think one look at that signature would tell you that. Not many subjects will give you a drawing to analyse as well. But that is another book.

> Pisces
>
> Certain routines or methods on the work front no longer serve any useful purpose, so you now have to make a number of decisive moves or maybe even burn a few bridges. However easy does it, because the Sun in Virgo after the 23rd means you must follow as well as lead.

Sample 2. Information: male, aged 26, right-handed, British.

Graphology

Sample 2

Optimistic. Extrovert. Independent. Emotionally detached. Concerned with spiritual matters. Can feel insecure. Idealistic. Logical thinker. Firm. Decisive. Controlled. Intuitive. Charming. Can be critical. Good attention to detail. Open. Speaks his mind. Could be blunt. Good at planning. Cautious. Industrious.

Well, how did you do?

Sample 2 was a computer systems analyst until fairly recently. He resigned to take up Zen Buddhism and yoga, both subjects he studies with an almost obsessional dedication. He is extremely health conscious. He spends a lot of time on his own, by choice, reading and studying. He has a very quick, sharp mind, a talent for making things and a very orderly, logical way about him. He has a good sense of humour.

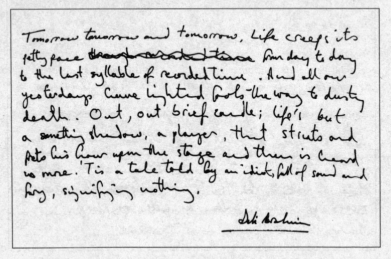

Sample 3. Information: male, aged 34, left-handed, British.

> The blueberry pancakes, served hot, with
> icecream melting inside them were
> the most delicious he had ever tasted.

Sample 4. Information: female, aged 19, right-handed, British.

> It is interesting to note that in British travellers'
> guides dating from the turn of the century, the
> recommended treatment for fatal snakebite in the
> bush is to explode a pinch of gunpowder over the
> wound or, if an extremity such as a finger or toe
> is bitten, to take a gun or light firearm and
> simply blow the extremity off.

Sample 5. Information: male, aged 56, right-handed, British.

> Kevin
>
> The genesis of this book was a desire to find
> out what were the effects on society of the most
> lethal disaster of recorded history – that is to
> say, of the black death of 1348-50, which killed
> an estimated one third of the population
> living between India and Iceland.

Sample 6. Information: male, aged 24, right-handed, British.

further reading

Branston, Barry, *Graphology Explained*, Piatkus Books, 1989

Cameron, Ellen, *An Introduction to Graphology*, The Aquarian Press, 1989

Gullan-Whur, Margaret, *What Your Handwriting Reveals*, Aquarian Press, 1984

Marley, John, *Graphology, Your Character in Your Handwriting*, Bancroft, 1967

Marne, Patricia, *Graphology*, Teach Yourself/Hodder & Stoughton, 1980

Marne, Patricia, *Understanding your Child's Writings and Drawings*, Optima, 1991

Singer, Eric, *A Manual of Graphology*, Duckworth, 1969

The Diagram Group, *The Complete Book of Predictions*, Panther Books, 1984

Wonder, Fritz, *Handwriting Analysis at Work*, Harper Collins, 1993

useful addresses

The Graphology Society, 33 Bonningtons, Thriftwood, Brentwood CM13 2TZ.

The British Institute of Graphologists, 4th Floor, Bell Court House, 11 Blumfield Street, London EC2 M7AY.

The Association for Graphological Studies, U.S.A., c/o Marion Rayner, Bermuda Lodge, Curley Hill Road, Lightwater, Surrey GU18 5YH. (Marion also runs a Handwriting Analysis Correspondence Course, write for details.)

The International Graphoanalysis Society, UK, Stonedge, Dunkerton, Bath BA2 8AS. (Correspondence course also available, write for details.)